SOCIAL MEDIA PLANNER & GUIDE 2022

Louise McDonnell

Published by Orla Kelly Publishing.

Hi,

Thank you for choosing to use my 2022 social media planner and guide. I wish you happiness and success in 2022.

I'm delighted to offer you some additional free online resources to help you with your social media planning including excel templates populated with over 400 prompts that you will find in this planner, hashtag groups by sector, organic post calculators, return on ad spend calculator and lots more! There is also a free video tutorial on how to get the most from this planner. You can access these resources at www.louisemcdonnell.com/2022resources

I'd also like to invite you to join me for a free live Masterclass on Sunday the 13th of February 2022 at 7pm GMT where I will look towards 2022 and give you lots of ideas for your social media content and ads.

I'd love to connect with you on social! You'll find me at @louisemcdsocial across all the social media platforms! If you are sharing pictures of my planner be sure to tag me and to use the hashtag #Kickstart2022

To your success,

Louise McDonnell
www.SellOnSocial.Media
www.louisemcdonnell.com

Personal Details

Name:

Address:

Email:

In an emergency please contact

Name:

Address:

Telephone:

Mobile:

Passwords

Brand Colours

Company Registration Number

Tax Reference Number

Vat Number

Tax Clearance Reference

Notes

CONTENTS

FREE SOCIAL MEDIA RESOURCES

Log on to claim your library of free resources which can be used hand in hand with this planner. Planning just became even easier with our monthly excel templates populated with over 400 social media prompts, content planning templates, hashtag libraries by sector, organic reach calculators, return on ad spend calculator, free video tutorials & much more...

www.louisemcdonnell.com/2022resources

MASTERCLASS

2022 Social Media Content Masterclass

€149 **FREE – To claim your free seat visit www.louisemcdonnell.com/2022resources**
Live on Sunday 13th February 2022 at 7pm GMT

In this masterclass, I will take you through the steps you need to create a year long content plan for your business. Learn:

1 **Trends** – what to expect in 2022

2 **A Proven 6 Step System to Guarantee Results** - The 6 step system I have created which gets quantifiable results fast. Whether you want to attract quality leads or generate online sales - this system works.

3 **Case Studies of Businesses that are Succeeding**

4 **Social Media Content** - We will look at the strategic role social media content plays in growing brand awareness and sales. Most people don't realize the link between content and sales.

5 **Tracking, Reporting, & Growing** - I will demystify how to interpret if a Facebook Ad is working. I'll include examples from product and service based companies in non-technical practical language.

Big Themes for 2022

Diversity & Inclusivity Matters

In March 2021 Facebook produced a report on, "The Difference Diversity Makes in Online Advertising". An analysis of 1022 global Facebook video ads found that limiting and negative representations are still present in online advertising. Women are 14 times more likely to be shown in revealing clothing and people with disabilities were only represented in 1.1% of ads analysed.

A survey commissioned by Facebook and carried out by Ipsos on 1,200 people aged 18 and older in Brazil, the United Kingdom and the United States found that 54% of consumers do not feel fully culturally represented in online advertising and 71% expect brands to promote diversity and inclusion in their online advertising.

In 2022 consider how your brand can play its role in promoting diversity and inclusivity in its social media strategy. Choose models and images for social media content and ads with purpose. Using video captions and image captions (Alt text) assists people with visual impairments. Be mindful also when using emojis and special characters as they reduce the user experience for people using VoiceOver and other assistive tools.

Augmented Reality for Business

Augmented reality filters are widely used by millions of people every day on platforms like Instagram, TikTok and Snapchat. Consumers love it and it keeps them engaged and coming back for more! Applying photo filters, adding sunglasses or even rabbits' ears are commonplace. Now, however we are seeing brands using augmented reality to interact with consumers in a new way. In 2013 IKEA, an early adopter of augmented reality ads released its iOS AR mobile app that showed users virtual pieces of furniture. The app allowed customers to see what a certain piece of furniture would look like in their homes therefore making it easier to make purchasing decisions. This emerging technology presents an amazing opportunity for changing the way businesses operate, communicate, and sell.

Eco-Consciousness

A 2020 global survey by Accenture found that 60% of those surveyed reported making more environmentally friendly, sustainable, or ethical purchases since the start of the pandemic. The survey also found that nine out of 10 said they were likely to continue doing so. A study conducted by GWI Zeitgeist in January 2021 examined the eco steps consumers most want brands to take. 52% of those surveyed said they wanted products with less packaging or recycled packaging. 48% wanted more affordable eco-friendly products, 44% wanted more natural ingredients, 43% wanted assistance with disposing of products, 36% wanted more transparency with sustainable practices and policies, 29% wanted to see donations to environmental groups or causes and 28% wanted to see brands partner with local environmental groups. Can you adopt any of these environmentally friendly policies? And if you do – be sure to let people know through your social media content and ads.

Shop Local

Supporting local retailers became a theme which emerged from the lockdowns of 2021. Google has reported that searches for "local" + "business(es)" have grown by more than 80% year on year, including searches like "local businesses near me" and "support local businesses". Social media, in particular Facebook, is a powerful channel for reaching local audiences either through organic content or paid ads. Fly your local flag, support local initiatives and do not forget to shout about it on your social media channels.

Online Shopping

The global e-commerce market is expected to be $5.9tn by the end of 2022. Shopify has reported that the pandemic has accelerated the shift to online shopping by as much as five years. According to Statistica, three out of four consumers say they buy from their smartphones because it saves time. The pandemic has also sped up consumers' adoption of real-time payment options by 41%. Real-time payment refers to digital wallet options where they can make payments quickly, such as Apple Pay, Google Pay, and PayPal.

According to GlobalWebIndex, 54% of social media users use social media to research products and 71% are more likely to purchase products and services based on social media referrals. According to a Deloitte report, 29% of social media users are more likely to make a purchase on the same day of seeing it on social media.

Simply having an e-commerce website and using social media alone will not deliver online sales. A solid social media strategy is required.

Privacy

The iOS Att Prompt which came into effect in Spring 2021 offered Apple users an easy way to opt out of being tracked online. This trend is set to continue in 2022 with Google announcing that it would end support to third-party cookies in their Chrome browser in 2022 which accounts for 70% of all internet browsing. This shift towards more privacy limits customer tracking and presents challenges to digital marketers. Now more than ever, it is important to grow your email list. You own your list and can control when you use it. Social media in app ads and content such as lead form ads and video view audiences will also become more important for building warm remarketing audiences.

Remote Working

Before the pandemic remote working was a novelty; now it is becoming the norm. According to a report by Forbes, by 2025, an estimated 70% of the workforce will be working remotely at least five days a month. In May 2021 Twitter told San Francisco based employees that they could work from home indefinitely. In its State of Remote Work survey, social media management company Buffer found that 99% of remote workers would like to continue working remotely at least part of the time for the rest of their careers, and 95% would recommend it to others. When people are working remotely they are more likely to be checking their social media at break time so this may impact the times of the day at which you post. Running lunch time webinars, tutorials or informational style posts will also appeal to remote workers. Social media helps bring people together even when they are physically apart. Consider how can you best connect with your potential customers who may be feeling more isolated working from home.

SOCIAL MEDIA CHANNELS

Facebook

About Set up in 2004, Facebook provides a platform for users around the world to connect with friends, family, communities and businesses. It is also the largest social networking site based on global reach and active users.

Users 2.85 billion active users.

What Makes Facebook Different?

Facebook is still the most popular social media platform on the planet. In my opinion what drives this is "personal connections". People connect with friends (from their youth, school and college days, workplaces, neighbours, etc.), family (first cousins, second cousins, aunts, uncles etc.) and through shared interests (generally through private groups).

For many of these relationships, Facebook and Messenger are the only places where communications and interactions take place. For example - if you want to check in with your cousins on the other side of the globe, or your friend from college who is celebrating their birthday – Facebook may be the only place or the easiest place to do this. Facebook is a network of worldwide personal connections. That is what keeps people coming back to it. While people may also be active on other social media platforms, chances are they are also active on Facebook too.

For many of my agency and Sell on Social Media Academy clients, Facebook is the number one platform for driving sales.

Predictions for 2022

Facebook Live

Facebook Live gives you the opportunity to use your Facebook page or group as your TV station! When you broadcast live you attract more viewers who are likely to spend three times longer watching your broadcast. Facebook Live broadcasts increased by 26.8% year on year in 2020 and this trend is set to continue in 2022.

 Use Streamyard.com to host interviews, webinars or online events.

Short-form Video

In 2021 we saw a trend towards short-form video with animations, like a twinkling star, flashing text, or a moving element in the background. These "Reel" or "TikTok" style videos perform well organically and as part of paid promotions.

Private Communities

The trend of creating private communities on Facebook has continued in 2021 and is set to continue in 2022. More than 1.8 billion people use Groups every month. These are active communities where people come together through shared interests, to learn new things, be entertained and make connections. Brands can create a group to facilitate user generated content or to offer exclusive content.

iOS 14 Prompt

The iOS 14 ATT Prompt which came into effect in Spring 2021 caused consternation in Facebook. The prompt enabled iOS mobile users to easily opt out of being tracked on apps and websites. This makes it harder to track Facebook Ad performance, to optimize for conversions and to grow website remarketing audiences. A trend emerging from this is towards more in App Ads which are unaffected by the prompt. Use "Video View Ads" to quickly grow warm remarketing audiences and "Lead Form Ads" for lead generation in app.

In App Shopping

According to a survey carried out by GlobalWebIndex in Q4 of 2020, social is now the number one discovery platform for finding new brands and products. Facebook and Instagram Shops provide an "always shopping" experience in app, which is curated based on shoppers preferences'. Online retailers will continue to embrace in app shopping in 2022 and can enhance the shopping experience by using collections, augmented reality and interactive live shopping experiences.

Business Messaging

Customers expect lightning-fast responses from businesses on Facebook. Chatbots can help you deliver the right answer the moment a customer asks. 70% of messages on Facebook are "pre-purchase", therefore responding by setting up automated responses is a tactic used to increase sales.

Hashtags

In September 2020, Facebook started to recommend including hashtags in posts to improve their discoverability. For example, including the hashtag, #socialmediaplanner in a post increases the chances of a post being discovered by someone that is not following you, but is following the newsfeed of that hashtag. I recommend using two or three hashtags per post; anymore can appear spammy.

Facebook Business Page

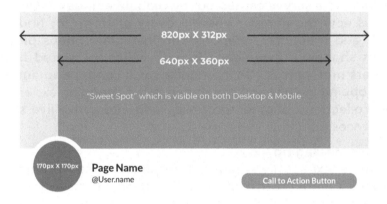

Profile Picture Size	170px x 170px Use the company logo or a professional headshot (for sole traders).
Cover Photo Size	Displays at 820 pixels wide by 312 pixels tall on your page on computers and 640 pixels wide by 360 pixels tall on smartphones.
Page Name	75 characters Use your company name – aim for consistency with your website and other social media channels.
Username Limit	50 characters Aim for consistency with other social media channels.
Description Limit	255 characters Remember to communicate your unique selling proposition here. Why should a prospective customer do business with you?
Post Limit	63,206 characters

Facebook Group Page

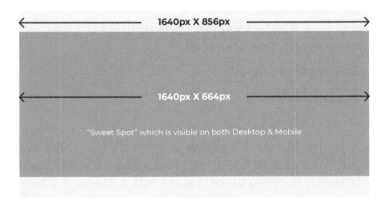

Facebook Event Page

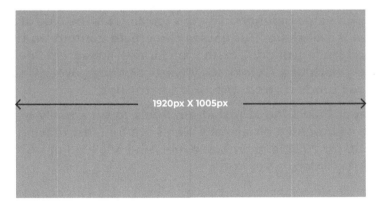

Instagram

About Launched in 2010, Instagram allows users to share videos and pictures with their audience.

Users 1.2 billion active users.

What Makes Instagram Different?

Instagram is the glossy magazine of the social media world. On Instagram it is all about "the look". Instagram is a mobile platform where, according to Head of Instagram Adam Mosseri, people come to be entertained. In June 2021 Mosseri spoke about building new features to enhance users' experience, with video being front and central to this approach. When planning Instagram content think entertainment, video, and mobile.

Links in posts are not functional – this too dictates the type of content that brands will share. Businesses can create content on the main news feed (gallery or grid), Instagram Stories, Instagram Reels (short fun style videos like TikTok), IGTV (vertical videos over 60 seconds) and upload products from their Instagram Shops.

Throughout 2021 I found Instagram Reels to be a really great way to reach new people organically. Reels are fun, fast moving videos. My top tip for 2022 is to embrace reels and any kind of fast moving entertaining video.

DIARY & CONTENT CALENDAR

Predictions for 2022

Instagram Stories

Considered to be Instagram's most popular features and one of parent company Facebook's best products. Over 500 million people use Instagram Stories daily. In 2020, 50% of influencer marketing campaigns used Instagram stories. In 2022 you should continue to embrace Instagram gifs, polls, Ask Me Anything and new features as they arrive.

The Rise of Reels
Instagram Reels were one of the hottest trends on Instagram in 2021. Reels are fun, fast moving, creative engaging videos. Businesses using "Creator" accounts on Instagram have access to trending chart music, but lose the ability to create video view audiences. If you want to increase organic reach in 2022, embrace Reels!

The Shopping Tab
70% of shoppers use Instagram for product discovery (Facebook, 2019). A shopping tab has made it easier for consumers to browse for products. Businesses that have set up their Instagram Shop can easily add links to where products can be purchased.

Visual Brand Storytelling
While this isn't a new trend, it still is as important as ever to know your brand essence and to communicate it effectively through your Instagram profile, highlights, and grid/gallery. The key to getting this right is planning in advance and this planner will help you do just that!

Profile Picture Size	180 x 180px ideal (110 x 110px minimum) Use the company logo or a professional headshot (for sole traders).
Username Limit	30 characters Aim for consistency across other social media platforms.
Bio Limit	150 characters Explain why people should follow your account and what they can expect. Why should potential customers do business with you? Use emojis to brighten up your bio!
Post Caption Limit	2200 characters
Square Newsfeed Photo	1080 x 1080px
Instagram Stories	1080 x 1920px

Twitter

About | Founded in 2006, Twitter is a 'microblogging' platform that allows users to send and receive short posts called tweets. It is estimated that 500 million tweets are sent daily.

Users | 192 million daily active users.

What Makes Twitter Different?

Twitter remains the number one dominant site for breaking news and trending news. You can often pick up a breaking news story on Twitter before the mainstream media picks it up.

Predictions for 2022

Engagement is still Queen
To get results on Twitter, brands must be active and willing to invest time engaging with their audiences using the platform. This trend will continue into 2022.

Video
According to a 2020 study by SocialPilot, up to 56% of video posts receive more engagement than other post types. Video Ads are also a great way to get your content in front of your audience. Twitter recommends keeping your video tweet copy short as it generates a 13% higher recall of your message and brand.

The use of Memes
Memes can be fun, inspirational or political and are popular with Twitter users who oftentimes reply to tweets with memes rather than words.

Infographics

Infographics are a great way to share a lot of information in a single image. This makes them popular with Twitter users as it encourages a lot of discussion.

Twitter Spaces

Rolled out in 2020, Spaces are live audio conversations on Twitter. On Twitter Mobile (iOS & Android), when someone you follow starts or speaks in a Space, it appears at the top of your timeline as a purple bubble for as long as it's live. Accounts with over 600 followers can host a Space. In 2022 embrace this new feature by hosting discussions, asking for feedback and hosting Q&As.

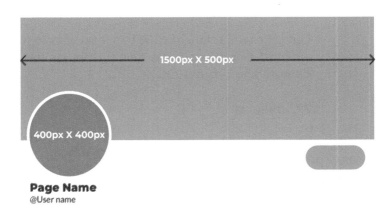

Page Name
@User name

Cover Photo Size (Header)	1500 x 500px
Profile Picture Size (Icon)	400 x 400px Use the company logo or a professional headshot (for sole traders).
Username Limit	15 characters Aim for consistency across other social media platforms.
Bio Limit	160 characters Explain why people should follow your account and what they can expect. Include a company hashtag if you have one.
Tweet Limit	280 characters

Linkedin

About   LinkedIn was set up in 2003 to allow users to network with other professionals and further develop their careers and reputations.

Users   722 million

What Makes Linkedin Different?

LinkedIn is the top business social network in the world. Use LinkedIn to connect with similar companies, suppliers, customers, and potential customers. Connect with people you studied with, worked with or have previously dealt with in the past. Set up a personal profile, business page, showcase pages, groups or events.

Predictions for 2022

Expansion of in-App Retargeting
In 2020 LinkedIn introduced retargeting of video viewers, Lead Gen Form openers and company page visitors. This kind of retargeting has been available on Facebook for years and is very effective at reaching warmer audiences.

Event Pages
LinkedIn Event pages were introduced in late 2019. Create an event by adding a description, date, time, a venue, and then invite your connections using filters such as location, company, industry, and school. LinkedIn Events are listed in your LinkedIn Page's "Events" tab; you can easily share the event with your page's followers or using InMail messages.

Linkedin Personal Profile

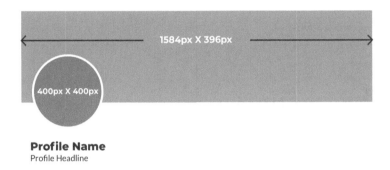

Profile Name
Profile Headline

Profile Picture Size	400 x 400px
Cover Image	1584 x 396px
Profile Name	Your name (and maiden name if relevant)
Headline	220 characters including spaces. Has a really prominent position on your profile and is used to index your profile for relevant searches.
Summary	2000 characters that have a very prominent position. Strike a balance between being general enough to cover your bases and specific enough to show up on search engines. Include keyword phrases – reinforce what is in your headline. On desktop the first 220 characters are immediately visible, with the rest requiring a user click on "View More". On mobile the first 92 characters are immediately visible.

Linkedin Company Page

Page Name
Page Category & Address

Page tagline

What makes your business different from others?

What can you say to stand out?)

Profile Image	300 x 300px
Cover Image	1128 x 191px
Page Tagline	220 characters Explain why people should follow your business page. What makes your business different from others? What can you say to stand out?
Company Name	100 characters
Company Description	2000 characters
Status Update Limit	700 characters

TikTok

About	Originally launched in 2014 as Musical.ly, TikTok is quickly becoming a popular form of user-generated content. Users can create, share and discover short videos such as singing, dancing and comedy content.
Users	1 billion

What Makes TikTok Different?

TikTok is all about short, fun, engaging video content. Predominantly used by young people to create videos with singing, lip syncing, dancing and having fun! Captions on posts are quite limited with just 100 characters to include hashtags and, similarly to Instagram, links to external websites do not work. If you tap into a trending theme it is possible to achieve high levels of organic reach through the discover tab. Using TikTok is a great way to improve your video creation skills! Embrace it!

Trends for 2022

Moving Mainstream
While it is the newish kid on the block, its popularity is growing phenomenally. As a brand it was front and central at the European Cup during the summer of 2021. It has also been used by global brands such as Universal Pictures and Shopify.

TikTok for Business
With the introduction of TikTok Business, we can expect to see an increase in the number of brands marketing on TikTok this year, particularly those targeting younger audiences. The Ad Creation process is very similar to creating Ads in the Facebook Business Manager. Worth checking out in 2022!

Influencer Marketing

According to a report published by Tribe Dynamics in 2020, 35% of influencers say they have started to use TikTok more frequently over the past year. The survey also reported that 35% of brands have a dedicated influencer marketing strategy and a team that focuses on just TikTok influencer marketing.

Profile Picture Size	20 x 20px
Video Size	1080 x 1920px
Bio Limit	80 characters
Username Limit	24 characters
Caption Limit	100 characters including hashtags

YouTube

About   YouTube was founded in 2005 and has since had 50 million users create, upload and share original video content. The platform also allows users to create their own profile, comment on other videos and subscribe to their favourite YouTubers.

Users: 1.86 billion

What Makes YouTube Different?

YouTube is like a library where all video content is stored and indexed. While other social media channels like Facebook and Instagram deliver higher levels of video viewers initially, YouTube will continue to deliver viewers for years to come – if the video is well optimised for relevant keywork phrases.

Predictions for 2022

Chapters

The Chapters feature enables viewers to select the section of a video they wish to watch. Similar to chapters on a book the viewer can easily see the content they wish to consume. Organising your video content in this way will increase video viewers.

YouTube Shorts

YouTube Shorts are 60-second vertical videos similar to TikTok. The platform was launched in September 2020 and has 6.5bn daily views globally. They are geared towards creators who want to produce short, snappy videos optimized for mobile.

Voice Search
YouTube users can now click on the microphone icon next to the search box to search for videos with their voice. When people use this function it tends to mean that they search by sentence rather than just phrases. To adapt when uploading your videos to YouTube do your keyword research and include long-tail keywords.

YouTube Channel

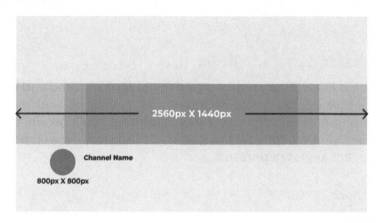

Profile Picture Size	800 x 800px
Channel Cover Image	2560 x 1440px
Username Limit	20 characters
Channel Description	1000 characters
Video Title Limit	70 characters
Video Description Limit	5000 characters

HOW TO CREATE A
SOCIAL MEDIA STRATEGY

The best way to spend less time producing better quality content is to plan ahead. Following these simple steps will assist you get better results from your social media marketing, no matter what social media channel you are using.

Here is a very simple guide to help you plan your social media and ads more effectively. I guarantee it will save you time and money. You will produce more effective, strategic content which will in turn enable you to run higher converting ad campaigns.

Step 1 Set Your SMART Goals

This is your starting point. The business goals you set for 2022 will greatly influence your social media content and ads. Failure to set goals often results in you wasting time and money on social media. If you do not know what you want to achieve you will simply meander along, with no purpose or direction and you may not make any progress.

Close your eyes and visualise what you want your business to look like this time next year. Think about what you would like to have achieved in the next 12 months - whether it is a particular sales or profit figure, the expansion of your workforce, increased confidence on social media or anything else you can think of.

What are 5 goals you would like your business to work towards this year?

This could be under the headings of finance, sales, marketing etc.

What will achieving your goals mean to you and your business?

By understanding the 'why' behind your goals, you are more likely to stay on track. Think about your 'why' every time you start to lose momentum.

What are you going to do between now and the end of the year to work towards achieving the goals and vision you have set out?

Break down your big goals into 'mini-goals' or weekly/daily actions to help you get another step further on your journey. Write these down in your planner to keep you on track.

Step 2   Why Should People do Business with You?

Why should potential customers choose you? What are your core messages and how can you differentiate yourself from your competitors in the eyes of your customer? It's important to dig deep into your business in this section.

What do you do?

Why did you start your company?/ Why was your organisation started?/What inspires you to do what you do?

What is special about your products/services?

Why do people choose you over your competitors?

What are the emotional reasons why people choose you?

Now...describe what you do...but integrate emotions, outcomes or fulfilment for your customer.

Step 3 Creating a Customer Focused Approach

Do you know why customers choose your products/services over your competitors? If you cannot clearly communicate how your business offering is different and why a potential customer should do business with you, then your social media content and ads will be less successful.

Create a Customer Persona/Avatar (for each product/service)

Who is your ideal customer?

> What is the typical age profile?

> What do they do?

> What are their interests?

> Where do they shop?

> What's important to them now in their lives?

What pain/need does your customer have? What are their frustrations? What words or phrases do they use to describe their situation?

What are the end results you achieve for your customers? How are their lives better after having purchased your products/services?

List 5 benefits of your product/service to your customer

Step 4 Creating a Content Plan

Understanding your customers is the key to successful content creation on social media, on your website and in all your marketing materials. In the last section we investigated who our customers are. We also considered the reasons that they choose to do business with us.

In this section we are going to start "having conversations" with our customers and potential customers on social media. We are going to visualize our typical customers and what we would say to them if they were sitting in front of us.

Social media is about connecting with our audience and consistently communicating our core messages to them.

The most important advice I can offer when it comes to creating social media content is.... it is not about what you want to say, it is about what your customer wants to hear about from you.

It is not about you. It is about them.

If you publish content that is useful to your customer, they are much more likely to engage.

A Marketing Channel
One of my favourite sayings is, "we sell more when we don't try to sell". We should see social media as a marketing channel rather than a sales channel. If we use social media as a sales channel only, we run the risk of continually running sales posts and ads. While this may work for some companies particularly targeting e-commerce sales, in general it is not a good strategy. Social media is a marketing channel where we can connect, communicate what is different about our brand and keep our brands top of mind. This is quite different than just selling.

 Feature you and your staff as much as possible in images and videos as this helps build brand awareness.

Brand Awareness Content

Sometimes we are connecting
This is generally the best performing content as it's engaging sociable content that your fans will interact with. It is not about selling; it is about getting your brand in front of customers and potential customers. Brand impressions are the aim here – how many times someone sees your logo, brand colours etc. The quality of your content and how much it appeals to your audiences will determine how they engage with it (likes, comment, tag friends, share). Make your audience feel like they know you. This helps build trust.
Examples of awareness content include,

- Behind the scenes
- Business milestones
- Funny Memes
- Inspirational Quotes
- Throwback images, etc.
- Employee feature
- Customer polls
- Customer generated content
- New stock arrivals
- Employee milestones
- Company milestones
- Industry updates
- Industry Trends
- News

Consideration Content

Sometimes we are building authority
This type of content enables your customers to connect with your brand in a more meaningful way. Consideration posts often offer advice or can be educational. How can you help your ideal customer right now? What advice can you give? Think about how you can position your company as an expert in the eyes of a potential customer.

Examples of awareness content include:

- Create a short video that solves a problem for your customer
- A "How To" post or video
- A product demonstration
- Industry trends
- Short webinar style videos
- Expert interviews
- Q&A
- Ask the Expert
- Answer FAQs

Conversion or Sales Content

Sometimes we are selling

These are posts where you sell a product or service. Sales posts should have a clear call to action (call now, email here, PM my page etc.) and should be directed at your warmest audiences. Use paid ads to get sales posts in front of people that have previously visited your website, watched your social media video content and follow you on Facebook & Instagram.

Advocate Content

Sometimes we are impressing

This is content produced by your most loyal customers. It is really valuable content as potential customers are more likely to believe what other people say about you rather than your own claims.

Encourage customers to post reviews/recommendations on your Facebook page, Google Map Listing, Website etc. Set up a system to encourage as many reviews as possible. Handpick people that you know will leave you a positive review. And... also ask for video reviews! You can use them as stand-alone content or create a collage of multiple testimonials!

Step 5   How to Maximize Reach on Social Media Posts

How you present your content on social media can have a big impact on organic reach. All social media platforms have algorithms which control content distribution. Algorithms favour content that has achieved engagement within a short time of being published. Think of "engagement" (likes, comments, views, clicks) as votes for your content.

Here are some pointers to consider every time you post:

Do

1. Think about the day and time of day to publish your post. Your audience needs to be there, but they also need to have time to *engage*.
2. Post eye catching graphics.
3. Use video as much as possible.
4. Post with purpose – make sure your post has purpose behind it and that you are not posting just for the sake of it or because it has been a few weeks since your last one.
5. Include **direct** product links to anything you post about which is available online or tell people how they can purchase it – make the buying decision easy for people instead of having them look all over for a product.
6. Mix up your content between awareness posts, consideration, sales and advocate content.
7. Think carefully about your post description – this will have a big impact on whether people engage or not.
8. Give your audience one call to action and one direction to follow.
9. Use hashtags to reach new people.

Avoid

1. Text only posts – always use an image. It is more likely that someone will skip by your post if you do not have an image or video.
2. Uploading videos that are too long or slow moving.
3. Sharing posts onto your business page from other business pages on Facebook – this lowers the organic reach and performance of your page.
4. Putting up a post of a product/service without telling people how they can find out more information and/or buy – you want to make it easier for someone to avail of your product/service.
5. Posting content that is trying to sell all the time - sales posts tend to have the lowest reach.
6. Do not just include the features of the product/service – think about the benefits.
7. Do not give your audience too many links or call to actions, you will confuse them.
8. Do not use too many hashtags on Facebook; they can look spammy.

Step 6 Augment Organic Reach with Paid Ads

Paid advertising not only allows us to reach more people – it also enables us to control who we reach.

As organic reach is often sporadic in nature, we cannot depend on it to grow sales and generate leads. It is therefore essential, no matter what social media channel you are using to have a budget to use on Paid Ads.

In section 3 we considered the profile of your ideal customer and created a "customer persona". This profiling will assist us target cold prospects that match the profile of your ideal customer.

We can also create warm "retargeting" audiences to reach people who appear, through actions they have taken, to be interested in your products and services. Examples of these actions include people who -

- Have visited your website
- Have taken specific actions on your website (e.g. Added to Cart, Purchased etc.)
- Are on your mailing list
- Have spent time watching your videos on social media
- Have interacted with your social media channels or ads in some way.

Conversion or Sales Content

It is so important when creating your ad to choose your headline and ad description well.

- Select an image or video thumbnail that will quickly get the attention of your ideal customer
- The headline should sell the benefits or your product/service. Focus on the outcome for the customer.
- Outline what problem you are solving or need that you are fulfilling?
- Incentivise the reader to act quickly by offering a limited time offer or restricted availability
- Add credibility by including examples of awards, accolades or social proof.
- Customer testimonials demonstrate how your product/service has worked for others
- Include one clear "call to action" (call now, email now, shop now etc.).

Step 7 Review Performance to Inform Future Campaigns

By tuning into how our organic content and paid ads are working we can gain an understanding of what is working and appealing to our audience.

Here are some common metrics to note:

Reach The number of people who saw your ad

Impressions The number of times your post or ad was viewed. If one person saw your post/ad 10 times, that would be 10 impressions and one reach.

Cost per Result The average cost you paid for each action (the action relates to the campaign objective. For example, if the campaign objective is to get purchases on your e-commerce website, the cost per result is how much each purchase cost you).

Budget	The maximum amount you are willing to pay for each ad set or campaign.
Clicks	Clicks on a post or ad.
CTR	Click through rate (The number of clicks divided by the number of impressions).
CPC	Cost per click.

For organic content tune into factors such as:

- Time of day
- Days of week
- Media used
- Type of post (meme, product demo etc.)
- Post description
- Hashtags
- Call to action

For paid advertising there are additional factors to consider including

- Campaign objective
- Audience selected
- Placement
- Schedule
- Media (image/video)
- Ad Copy
- Call to action
- Landing page
- Offer
- Reputation

HOW TO USE THIS CONTENT CALENDAR

This social media content calendar will help you organise your social media content and campaign in advance. When you plan in advance, you take the pressure off and have more time to be creative. Planning in advance will save you time and you are more likely to produce better quality content.

Get into the routine of setting some time aside to plan and work on your social media content.

Use the prompts in this section to give you inspiration for your social media posts. Consider how you can make the prompt relevant to your business.

Some of the prompts are fun and will help you with your awareness content (see step 4 in the previous section). Others you can use to position your business and demonstrate your knowledge.

Remember to include the hashtags in your posts. This assists your content to be discovered by people who may not be following you, but may be following the newsfeed of that hashtag.

These prompts are taken from all over the world and will give you the opportunity to achieve a global reach.

JANUARY 2022

Veganuary / #Veganuary
Dry January / #DryJanuary

Date	Day	#
Sat 01	New Year's Day	#NewYears
Sun 02	National Buffet Day	#BuffetDay
Mon 03	Festival of Sleep Day	#FestivalofSleepDay
Tue 04	National Trivia Day World Braille Day	#NationalTriviaDay #WorldBrailleDay
Wed 05	National Whipped Cream Day	#NationalWhippedCreamDay
Thur 06	National Bean Day National Technology Day	#NationalBeanDay #NationalTechnologyDay
Fri 07	National Tempura Day	#TempuraDay
Sat 08	National Bubble Bath Day	#NationalBubbleBathDay
Sun 09	National Apricot Day	#NationalApricotDay
Mon 10	National Clean Your Desk Day National Cut Your Energy Costs Day	#CleanOffYourDeskDay #CutYourEnergyCostsDay
Tue 11	National Human Trafficking Awareness Day	#HumanTrafficking AwarenessDay
Wed 12	National Pharmacist Day	#NationalPharmacistDay
Thur 13	National Sticker Day	#NationalStickerDay
Fri 14	National Dress Up Your Pet Day	#DressUpYourPetDay

Date	Day	#
Sat 15	National Hat Day	#NationalHatDay
Sun 16	World Snow Day World Religion Day	#SnowDay #ReligionDay
Mon 17	Martin Luther King Day	#MLKDay
Tue 18	National Thesaurus Day	#NationalThesaurusDay
Wed 19	National Popcorn Day	#NationalPopcornDay
Thur 20	National Penguin Day Get to Know Your Customers Day	#NationalPenguinDay #GetToKnowYourCustomersDay
Fri 21	National Hugging Day	#NationalHuggingDay
Sat 22	Celebration of Life Day	#CelebrationofLifeDay
Sun 23	National Handwriting Day	#NationalHandwritingDay
Mon 24	National Compliment Day	#NationalComplimentDay
Tue 25	Opposite Day National Irish Coffee Day	#OppositeDay #NationalIrishCoffeeDay
Wed 26	National Spouses Day	#NationalSpousesDay #SpousesDay
Thur 27	Holocaust Memorial Day	#HolocaustMemorialDay
Fri 28	Data Privacy Day	#PrivacyAware
Sat 29	National Puzzle Day	#NationalPuzzleDay
Sun 30	National Croissant Day	#NationalCroissantDay
Mon 31	National Hot Chocolate Day	#NationalHotChocolateDay

JANUARY 2022

Sun	Mon	Tue	Wed	Thu	Fri	Sat
						01
02	03	04	05	06	07	08
09	10	11	12	13	14	15
16	17	18	19	20	21	22
23	24	25	26	27	28	29
30	31					

> Notes

FEBRUARY 2022

Black History Month / #BlackHistoryMonth

Date	Day	#
Tue 01	National Freedom Day Chinese New Year	#NationalFreedomDay #ChineseNewYear #YearOfTheTiger
Wed 02	Groundhog Day World Wetlands Day	#GroundhogDay #WorldWetlandsDay
Thur 03	National Golden Retriever Day	#NationalGoldenRetrieverDay
Fri 04	World Cancer Day	#WorldCancerDay #WeCanICan
Sat 05	World Nutella Day	#WorldNutellaDay
Sun 06	National Time To Talk Day	#TimeToTalk
Mon 07	National Send A Card To A Friend Day	#SendACardToAFriendDay
Tue 08	Safer Internet Day	#SaferInternetDay
Wed 09	National Pizza Day	#NationalPizzaDay
Thur 10	National Umbrella Day	#NationalUmbrellaDay
Fri 11	World Day of the Sick	#WorldDayoftheSick
Sat 12	National Freedom To Marry Day	#NationalFreedomToMarryDay
Sun 13	World Radio Day	#WorldRadioDay
Mon 14	Valentine's Day	#ValentinesDay

Date	Day	#
Tue 15	Singles Awareness Day	#SinglesAwarenessDay
Wed 16	National Almond Day	#AlmondDay
Thur 17	Random Acts of Kindness Day	#RandomActsOfKindnessDay #RAKDay
Fri 18	National Drink Wine Day	#NationalDrinkWineDay
Sat 19	Tug Of War Day	#TugOfWarDay
Sun 20	World Day of Social Justice National Love Your Pet Day	#SocialJusticeDay #LoveYourPetDay
Mon 21	Presidents Day International Mother Language Day	#PresidentsDay #MotherLanguageDay
Tue 22	National Margarita Day	#NationalMargaritaDay
Wed 23	National Banana Bread Day	#NationalBananaBreadDay
Thur 24	National Tortilla Chip Day National Toast Day	#NationalTortillaChipDay #NationalToastDay
Fri 25	National Skip the Straw Day	#NationalSkipTheStrawDay
Sat 26	National Pistachio Day	#NationalPistachioDay
Sun 27	International Polar Bear Day	#InternationalPolarBearDay
Mon 28	National Public Sleeping Day	#NationalPublicSleepingDay

FEBRUARY 2022

Sun	Mon	Tue	Wed	Thu	Fri	Sat
		01	02	03	04	05
06	07	08	09	10	11	12
13	14	15	16	17	18	19
20	21	22	23	24	25	26
27	28					

> Notes

MARCH 2022

Women's History Month / #WomensHistoryMonth

Date	Day	#
Tue 01	Self-Injury Awareness Day Pancake Tuesday	#SIAD #PancakeTuesday
Wed 02	National Old Stuff Day Ash Wednesday	#NationalOldStuffDay #AshWednesday
Thur 03	World Wildlife Day	#WorldWildlifeDay
Fri 04	National Grammar Day Employee Appreciation Day	#NationalGrammarDay #EmployeeAppreciationDay
Sat 05	National Absinthe Day	#NationalAbsintheDay
Sun 06	National Oreo Cookie Day	#NationalOreoCookieDay
Mon 07	National Be Heard Day	#NationalBeHeardDay
Tue 08	International Women's Day	#InternationalWomensDay
Wed 09	National Get Over It Day National Barbie Day	#NationalGetOverItDay #BarbieDay
Thur 10	National Pack Your Lunch Day World Kidney Day	#PackYourLunchDay #WorldKidneyDay
Fri 11	National Funeral Director and Mortician Day	#NationalFuneralDirectorDay
Sat 12	National Plant A Flower Day	#NationalPlantAFlowerDay
Sun 13	National Good Samaritan Day	#GoodSamaritanDay
Mon 14	National Napping Day National Potato Chip Day	#NationalNappingDay #NationalPotatoChipDay

Date	Day	#
Tue 15	World Consumer Rights Day World Social Work Day	#WCRD2022 #WorldSocialWorkDay
Wed 16	National Panda Day	#NationalPandaDay
Thur 17	Saint Patrick's Day	#StPatricksDay
Fri 18	Global Recycling Day	#GlobalRecyclingDay
Sat 19	National Poultry Day	#NationalPoultryDay
Sun 20	International Day of Happiness First Day of Spring	#InternationalDayOfHappiness #FirstDayOfSpring
Mon 21	World Down Syndrome Day	#WDSD #WorldDownSyndromeDay
Tue 22	World Water Day	#WorldWaterDay
Wed 23	World Meteorological Day National Puppy Day	#WorldMeteorologicalDay #NationalPuppyDay
Thur 24	World Tuberculosis Day	#WorldTuberculosisDay
Fri 25	International Waffle Day	#InternationalWaffleDay
Sat 26	National Spinach Day	#NationalSpinachDay
Sun 27	World Theatre Day UK and Ireland Mother's Day	#WorldTheatreDay #MothersDay #MothersDay2022
Mon 28	Respect Your Cat Day	#RespectYourCatDay
Tue 29	National Vietnam War Veterans Day	#VietnamWarVeteransDay #VietnamVeterans
Wed 30	Take a Walk in the Park Day	#TakeAWalkInTheParkDay
Thur 31	National Crayon Day	#NationalCrayonDay

MARCH 2022

Sun	Mon	Tue	Wed	Thu	Fri	Sat
		01	02	03	04	05
06	07	08	09	10	11	12
13	14	15	16	17	18	19
20	21	22	23	24	25	26
27	28	29	30	31		

> Notes

APRIL 2022

Autism Awareness Month / #AutismAwarenessMonth

Date	Day	#
Fri 01	April Fool's Day	#AprilFoolsDay
Sat 02	World Autism Awareness Day	#WorldAutismAwarenessDay
Sun 03	National Find a Rainbow Day	#NationalFindARainbowDay
Mon 04	International Day for Landmine Awareness	#InternationalMineAwareness
Tue 05	Gold Star Spouses Day	#GoldStarSpouses
Wed 06	International Day of Sport for Development and Peace	#IDSDP #WhiteCard
Thur 07	World Health Day	#WorldHealthDay
Fri 08	National Zoo Lovers Day	#ZooLoversDay
Sat 09	National Unicorn Day	#NationalUnicornDay
Sun 10	National Siblings Day	#NationalSiblingsDay
Mon 11	National Pet Day	#NationalPetDay
Tue 12	National Grilled Cheese Day International Day of Human Space Flight	#NationalGrilledCheeseDay #HumanSpaceFlight
Wed 13	National Scrabble Day	#NationalScrabbleDay
Thur 14	National Dolphin Day	#NationalDolphinDay

Date	Day	#
Fri 15	World Art Day Good Friday	#WorldArtDay #GoodFriday
Sat 16	Husband Appreciation Day	#HusbandAppreciationDay
Sun 17	Easter Sunday	#EasterSunday
Mon 18	National Columnists Day	#ColumnistsDay
Tue 19	National Wear Your Pyjamas to Work Day	#PJDay
Wed 20	National Lookalike Day	#NationalLookalikeDay
Thur 21	World Creativity and Innovation Day National High Five Day	#WorldCreativityAndInnovationDay #NationalHighFiveDay
Fri 22	Earth Day	#EarthDay
Sat 23	National Picnic Day	#PicnicDay
Sun 24	Orthodox Easter National Pet Parents Day	#NationalPetParentsDay
Mon 25	World Penguin Day National Telephone Day	#WorldPenguinDay #NationalTelephoneDay
Tue 26	International Chernobyl Disaster Remembrance Day	#ChernobylDisasterDay
Wed 27	National Tell A Story Day	#NationalTellAStoryDay
Thur 28	World Day for Safety and Health at Work	#SafetyAndHealthAtWork
Fri 29	International Dance Day	#InternationalDanceDay
Sat 30	International Jazz Day	#InternationalJazzDay

 LouiseMcDonnell

APRIL 2022

Sun	Mon	Tue	Wed	Thu	Fri	Sat
					01	02
03	04	05	06	07	08	09
10	11	12	13	14	15	16
17	18	19	20	21	22	23
24	25	26	27	28	29	30

> Notes

MAY 2022

Cystic Fibrosis Awareness Month / #CFAwareness

Date	Day	#
Sun 01	May Day World Lyme Day World Laughter Day	#MayDay #WorldLymeDay #WorldLaughterDay
Mon 02	Astronomy Day International Harry Potter Day	#InternationalAstronomyDay #InternationalHarryPotterDay
Tue 03	World Press Freedom Day World Asthma Day	#WorldPressFreedomDay #WorldAsthmaDay
Wed 04	Star Wars Day	#StarWarsDay #MayThe4thBeWithYou
Thur 05	World Password Day	#WorldPasswordDay
Fri 06	National No Diet Day	#NoDietDay
Sat 07	Beaufort Scale Day	#BeaufortScaleDay
Sun 08	U.S. Mother's Day	#MothersDay
Mon 09	Europe Day	#EuropeDay
Tue 10	National Clean Your Room Day	#CleanUpYourRoomDay
Wed 11	National Receptionists Day	#NationalReceptionistsDay
Thur 12	International Nurses Day	#IND2022
Fri 13	International Hummus Day Friday the 13th	#HummusDay
Sat 14	World Fair Trade Day	#FairTradeDay

Date	Day	#
Sun 15	International Day of Families	#FamilyDay
Mon 16	International Day of Light	#DayOfLight
Tue 17	World Telecommunication and Information Society Day	#WTISD
Wed 18	International Museum Day National No Dirty Dishes Day	#MuseumDay #NationalNoDirtyDishesDay
Thur 19	World IBD Day	#WorldIBDDay2022
Fri 20	World Bee Day Bike to Work Day	#WorldBeeDay #BikeToWorkDay
Sat 21	World Day For Cultural Diversity	#WorldDayForCultural Diversity
Sun 22	International Day for Biological Diversity	#BiologicalDiversity
Mon 23	World Turtle Day	#WorldTurtleDay
Tue 24	National Brother's Day	#NationalBrothersDay
Wed 25	National Wine Day	#NationalWineDay
Thur 26	National Paper Airplane Day	#PaperAirplaneDay
Fri 27	National Sunscreen Day	#NationalSunscreenDay
Sat 28	National Hamburger Day	#NationalHamburgerDay
Sun 29	Learn About Composting Day	#LearnAboutCompostingDay
Mon 30	World MS Day	#WorldMSDay
Tue 31	World No Tobacco Day	#NoTobaccoDay

MAY 2022

Sun	Mon	Tue	Wed	Thu	Fri	Sat
01	02	03	04	05	06	07
08	09	10	11	12	13	14
15	16	17	18	19	20	21
22	23	24	25	26	27	28
29	30	31				

> Notes

JUNE 2022

Pride Month / #PrideMonth

Date	Day	#
Wed 01	Global Day of Parents Global Running Day	#GlobalDayOfParents #GlobalRunningDay
Thur 02	National Leave The Office Early Day	#LeaveTheOfficeEarlierDay
Fri 03	National Egg Day National Donut Day	#NationalEggDay #NationalDonutDay
Sat 04	National Cognac Day	#NationalCognacDay
Sun 05	World Environment Day	#WorldEnvironmentDay
Mon 06	D-Day Anniversary	#DDay
Tue 07	World Food Safety Day	#WorldFoodSafetyDay
Wed 08	World Oceans Day National Best Friend Day	#WorldOceansDay #NationalBestFriendDay
Thur 09	National Donald Duck Day	#NationalDonaldDuckDay
Fri 10	National Iced Tea Day	#NationalIcedTeaDay
Sat 11	World Gin Day	#WorldGinDay
Sun 12	World Day Against Child Labour	#AgainstChildLabour
Mon 13	International Albinism Awareness Day	#AlbinismAwarenessDay
Tue 14	World Blood Donor Day	#WorldBloodDonorDay

Date	Day	#
Wed 15	World Elder Abuse Awareness Day	#WorldElderAbuse AwarenessDay
Thur 16	Fresh Veggies Day	#FreshVeggiesDay
Fri 17	Eat Your Vegetables Day	#EatYourVegetablesDay
Sat 18	International Picnic Day	#InternationalPicnicDay
Sun 19	National Martini Day Fathers Day	#NationalMartiniDay #FathersDay
Mon 20	World Refugee Day	#WorldRefugeeDay
Tue 21	National Selfie Day	#NationalSelfieDay
Wed 22	World Rainforest Day	#WorldRainforestDay
Thur 23	United Nations Public Service Day	#UNPublicServiceDay
Fri 24	Take Your Dog to Work Day	#TakeYourDogToWorkDay
Sat 25	Global Beatles Day	#GlobalBeatlesDay
Sun 26	National Beautician's Day	#BeauticiansDay
Mon 27	National Sunglasses Day Micro-, Small and Medium-Sized Enterprises Day	#NationalSunglassesDay #MSMEDay22
Tue 28	National Insurance Awareness Day	#NationalInsurance AwarenessDay
Wed 29	National Camera Day	#NationalCameraDay
Thur 30	Social Media Day National Handshake Day	#SMDay #NationalHandshakeDay

JUNE 2022

Sun	Mon	Tue	Wed	Thu	Fri	Sat
			01	02	03	04
05	06	07	08	09	10	11
12	13	14	15	16	17	18
19	20	21	22	23	24	25
26	27	28	29	30		

> Notes

JULY 2022

Date	Day	#
Fri 01	Canada Day	#CanadaDay
Sat 02	World UFO Day	#WorldUFODay
Sun 03	International Plastic Bag Free Day	#InternationalPlasticBagFreeDay
Mon 04	Independence Day	#IndependenceDay
Tue 05	National Workaholics Day	#NationalWorkaholicsDay
Wed 06	International Kissing Day	#InternationalKissingDay
Thur 07	World Chocolate Day	#WorldChocolateDay
Fri 08	National Video Game Day	#NationalVideoGameDay
Sat 09	National Sugar Cookie Day	#NationalSugarCookieDay
Sun 10	National Pina Colada Day	#NationalPinaColadaDay
Mon 11	World Population Day	#WorldPopulationDay
Tue 12	National Pecan Pie Day	#NationalPecanPieDay
Wed 13	National French Fry Day	#NationalFrenchFryDay
Thur 14	Bastille Day National Mac and Cheese Day	#BastilleDay #MacAndCheeseDay

Date	Day	#
Fri 15	World Youth Skills Day	#WorldYouthSkillsDay
Sat 16	World Snake Day	#WorldSnakeDay
Sun 17	World Emoji Day	#WorldEmojiDay
Mon 18	Nelson Mandela International Day	#MandelaDay
Tue 19	Daiquiri Day	#NationalDaquiriDay
Wed 20	National Moon Day National Hot Dog Day	#MoonDay #NationalHotDogDay
Thur 21	National Junk Food Day	#NationalJunkFoodDay
Fri 22	National Hammock Day	#NationalHammockDay
Sat 23	National Gorgeous Grandma Day	#NationalGorgeousGrandmaDay
Sun 24	International Self Care Day	#SelfCareDay
Mon 25	National Wine And Cheese Day	#WineAndCheeseDay
Tue 26	Aunt And Uncle Day	#AuntAndUncleDay
Wed 27	Scotch Whisky Day	#NationalScotchDay
Thur 28	Chili Dog Day	#ChiliDogDay
Fri 29	National Lasagna Day National Intern Day	#NationalLasagnaDay #NationalInternDay
Sat 30	International Friendship Day National Cheesecake Day	#InternationalFriendshipDay #CheesecakeDay
Sun 31	National Avocado Day	#NationalAvocadoDay

JULY 2022

Sun	Mon	Tue	Wed	Thu	Fri	Sat
					01	02
03	04	05	06	07	08	09
10	11	12	13	14	15	16
17	18	19	20	21	22	23
24	25	26	27	28	29	30
31						

> Notes

AUGUST 2022

National Dog Month / #NationalDogMonth

Date	Day	#
Mon 01	National Girlfriend Day World Wide Web Day	#NationalGirlfriendDay #WorldWideWebDay
Tue 02	National Colouring Book Day	#NationalColouringBookDay
Wed 03	National Watermelon Day	#NationalWatermelonDay
Thur 04	National Chocolate Chip Cookie Day	#NationalChocolateChipDay
Fri 05	National Underwear Day International Beer Day	#NationalUnderwearDay #InternationalBeerDay
Sat 06	National Fresh Breath Day	#NationalFreshBreathDay
Sun 07	National Lighthouse Day	#NationalLighthouseDay
Mon 08	International Cat Day	#InternationalCatDay
Tue 09	National Book Lovers Day	#NationalBookLoversDay
Wed 10	National Lazy Day	#NationalLazyDay
Thur 11	National Son and Daughter Day	#SonAndDaughterday
Fri 12	World Elephant Day International Youth Day	#WorldElephantDay #InternationalYouthDay
Sat 13	International Left-Handers Day	#InternationalLeftHandersDay
Sun 14	World Lizard Day	#WorldLizardDay

Date	Day	#
Mon 15	National Relaxation Day	#NationalRelaxationDay
Tue 16	National Tell a Joke Day	#NationalTellAJokeDay
Wed 17	National Non-Profit Day	#NationalNonProfitDay
Thur 18	National Couple's Day	#NationalCouplesDay
Fri 19	World Humanitarian Day	#WorldHumanitarianDay
Sat 20	National Radio Day National Tooth Fairy Day	#NationalRadioDay #NationalToothFairyDay
Sun 21	Senior Citizens Day	#SeniorCitizensDay
Mon 22	Folklore Day Rainbow Baby Day	#FolkloreDay #RainbowBabyDay
Tue 23	National Sponge Cake Day	#NationalSpongeCakeDay
Wed 24	International Strange Music Day	#StrangeMusicDay
Thur 25	National Second Hand Wardrobe Day	#SecondHandWardrobeDay
Fri 26	National Dog Day	#NationalDogDay
Sat 27	National Just Because Day	#JustBecauseDay
Sun 28	National Bow Tie Day	#NationalBowTieDay
Mon 29	National Lemon Juice Day	#LemonJuiceDay
Tue 30	National Beach Day	#NationalBeachDay
Wed 31	National Matchmakers Day National Bacon Day	#NationalMatchmakersDay #NationalBaconDay

AUGUST 2022

Sun	Mon	Tue	Wed	Thu	Fri	Sat
	01	02	03	04	0	06
07	08	09	10	11	12	13
14	15	16	17	18	19	20
21	22	23	24	25	26	27
28	29	30	31			

> Notes

SEPTEMBER 2022

National Suicide Prevention Month
/ #NationalSuicidePreventionMonth

Date	Day	#
Thur 01	Letter Writing Day	#WorldLetterWritingDay
Fri 02	World Coconut Day	#CoconutDay
Sat 03	World Beard Day	#WorldBeardDay
Sun 04	Fathers Day (Australia)	#FathersDay
Mon 05	International Day of Charity	#InternationalDayOfCharity
Tue 06	Read a Book Day	#ReadABookDay
Wed 07	National Salami Day	#NationalSalamiDay
Thur 08	International Literacy Day	#InternationalLiteracyDay
Fri 09	National Teddy Bear Day	#NationalTeddyBearDay
Sat 10	World Suicide Prevention Day	#WorldSuicidePreventionDay
Sun 11	National Day of Service and Remembrance	#PatriotsDay
	National Grandparents Day US	#NationalGrandparentsDay
Mon 12	National Day Of Encouragement	#DayOfEncouragement
Tue 13	Positive Thinking Day	#PositiveThinkingDay
Wed 14	National Live Creative Day	#NationalLiveCreativeDay

Date	Day	#
Thur 15	International Day of Democracy	#InternationalDayOfDemocracy
Fri 16	National Guacamole Day	#NationalGuacamoleDay
Sat 17	National Clean Up Day	#NationalCleanUpDay
Sun 18	European Heritage Days	#EuropeanHeritageDays
Mon 19	International Talk Like a Pirate Day	#InternationalTalkLikeAPirateDay
Tue 20	National Pepperoni Pizza Day	#NationalPepperoniPizzaDay
Wed 21	International Day of Peace	#PeaceDay
Thur 22	World Rhino Day	#WorldRhinoDay
Fri 23	Beginning of Autumn International Day of Sign Languages	#Autumn #InternationalDayOfSign Languages
Sat 24	Punctuation Day	#PunctuationDay
Sun 25	Comic Book Day National Day Of Cooking	#NationalComicBookDay #NationalCookingDay
Mon 26	National Family Day	#FamilyDay
Tue 27	World Tourism Day	#WorldTourismDay
Wed 28	World Rabies Day	#WorldRabiesDay
Thur 29	National Coffee Day	#NationalCoffeeDay
Fri 30	International Podcast Day	#InternationalPodcastDay

SEPTEMBER 2022

Sun	Mon	Tue	Wed	Thu	Fri	Sat
				01	02	03
04	05	06	07	08	09	10
11	12	13	14	15	16	17
18	19	20	21	22	23	24
25	26	27	28	29	30	

> Notes

OCTOBER 2022

Breast Awareness Month / #BreastAwarenessMonth

Date	Day	#
Sat 01	World Vegetarian Day International Coffee Day	#WorldVegetarianDay #InternationalCoffeeDay
Sun 02	International Day Of Non-Violence	#InternationalDayOf Non-Violence
Mon 03	National Boyfriend Day	#NationalBoyfriendDay
Tue 04	National Taco Day	#NationalTacoDay
Wed 05	World Teachers Day	#WorldTeachersDay
Thur 06	International Walk to School Day	#WalkToSchoolDay
Fri 07	National Body Language Day	#NationalBodyLanguageDay
Sat 08	National Chess Day	#NationalChessDay
Sun 09	World Post Day	#WorldPostDay
Mon 10	World Mental Health Day	#WorldMentalHealthDay
Tue 11	International Day Of The Girls	#DayOfTheGirl
Wed 12	National Stop Bullying Day	#NationalStopBullyingDay
Thur 13	National Train Your Brain Day	#TrainYourBrainDay
Fri 14	National Dessert Day	#DessertDay

Date	Day	#
Sat 15	Global Handwashing Day	#GlobalHandwashingDay
Sun 16	World Food Day Boss's Day	#WorldFoodDay #BosssDay
Mon 17	National Pasta Day	#NationalPastaDay
Tue 18	National No-Beard Day	#NationalNoBeardDay
Wed 19	National New Friends Day	#NationalNewFriendsDay
Thur 20	International Chefs Day	#InternationalChefsDay
Fri 21	International Day Of The Nacho	#InternationalDayOfTheNacho
Sat 22	National Nut Day	#NationalNutDay
Sun 23	National Mother-In-Law Day	#MotherInLawDay
Mon 24	United Nations Day	#UnitedNationsDay
Tue 25	International Artists Day	#InternationalArtistsDay
Wed 26	National Pumpkin Day	#NationalPumpkinDay
Thur 27	National Mentoring Day World Occupational Therapy Day	#NationalMentoringDay #WorldOTDay
Fri 28	National Chocolate Day	#NationalChocolateDay
Sat 29	World Stroke Day	#WorldStrokeDay
Sun 30	National Checklist Day	#ChecklistDay
Mon 31	Halloween	#Halloween

 **LouiseMcDonnell**

OCTOBER 2022

Sun	Mon	Tue	Wed	Thu	Fri	Sat
						01
02	03	04	05	06	07	08
09	10	11	12	13	14	15
16	17	18	19	20	21	22
23	24	25	26	27	28	29
30	31					

> Notes

NOVEMBER 2022

Men's Health Awareness Month / #Movember

Date	Day	#
Tue 01	National Author's Day World Vegan Day	#NationalAuthorsDay #WorldVeganDay
Wed 02	All Souls Day International Stress Awareness Day	#AllSoulsDay #StressAwarenessDay
Thur 03	National Men Make Dinner Day	#NationalMenMakeDinnerDay
Fri 04	National Candy Day	#NationalCandyDay
Sat 05	American Football Day	#AmericanFootballDay
Sun 06	National Saxophone Day	#NationalSaxophoneDay
Mon 07	Job Action Day	#JobActionDay
Tue 08	National Cappuccino Day	#NationalCappuccinoDay
Wed 09	World Adoption Day	#WorldAdoptionDay
Thur 10	World Science Day for Peace and Development	#WorldScienceDay #WSDPD
Fri 11	Veterans Day	#VeteransDay
Sat 12	World Pneumonia Day	#WorldPnuemoniaDay
Sun 13	World Kindness Day	#WorldKindnessDay
Mon 14	World Diabetes Day	#WorldDiabetesDay

Date	Day	#
Tue 15	Clean Out Your Fridge Day	#CleanYourFridge
Wed 16	National Fast Food Day	#NationalFastFoodDay
Thur 17	National Take A Hike Day	#TakeAHikeDay
Fri 18	National Princess Day	#NationalPrincessDay
Sat 19	International Mens Day	#InternationalMensDay
Sun 20	International Childrens Day	#WorldChildrensDay
Mon 21	World Television Day World Hello Day	#TelevisionDay #WorldHelloDay
Tue 22	Go For A Ride Day	#GoForARideDay
Wed 23	National Espresso Day	#NationalEspressoDay
Thur 24	Thanksgiving Day	#Thanksgiving
Fri 25	Black Friday	#BlackFriday
Sat 26	National Cake Day	#NationalCakeDay
Sun 27	First Day of Advent	#Advent
Mon 28	Cyber Monday	#CyberMonday
Tue 29	National Day of Giving Electronic Greetings Day	#NationalDayOfGiving #ElectronicGreetingsDay
Wed 30	International Computer Security Day	#ComputerSecurityDay

NOVEMBER 2022

Sun	Mon	Tue	Wed	Thu	Fri	Sat
		01	02	03	04	05
06	07	08	09	10	11	12
13	14	15	16	17	18	19
20	21	22	23	24	25	26
27	28	29	30			

> Notes

DECEMBER 2022

Universal Human Rights Month
/ #HumanRightsMonth

Date	Day	#
Thur 01	National Christmas Lights Day World AIDS Day	#NationalChristmasLightsDay #WorldAIDSDay #WAD2022
Fri 02	Bartender Appreciation Day	#BartenderAppreciationDay
Sat 03	International Day of Persons with Disabilities	#IDPD
Sun 04	National Candy Day	#NationalCandyDay
Mon 05	International Volunteer Day	#InternationalVolunteerDay
Tue 06	Saint Nicholas Day	#StNicholasDay
Wed 07	National Letter Writing Day	#NationalLetterWritingDay
Thur 08	National Brownie Day	#NationalBrownieDay
Fri 09	National Anti-Corruption Day	#UnitedAgainstCorruptionDay
Sat 10	Human Rights Day	#HumanRightsDay
Sun 11	International Mountain Day	#InternationalMountainDay
Mon 12	National Poinsettia Day	#PoinsettiaDay
Tue 13	Day of the Horse	#DayOfTheHorse
Wed 14	National Free Online Shipping Day	#FreeShipping

Date	Day	#
Thur 15	International Tea Day	#InternationalTeaDay
Fri 16	National Ugly Sweater Day	#NationalUglySweaterDay
Sat 17	National Maple Syrup Day	#MapleSyrupDay
Sun 18	International Migrants Day	#InternaitonalMigrantsDay
Mon 19	National Emo Day	#NationalEmoDay
Tue 20	International Human Solidarity Day	#HumanSolidarityDay
Wed 21	Winter Solstice	#WinterSolstice
Thur 22	National Short Person Day	#NationalShortPersonDay
Fri 23	National Roots Day	#NationalRootsDay
Sat 24	Christmas Eve Last Day of Advent	#ChristmasEve #LastDayofAdvent
Sun 25	Christmas Day	#MerryChristmas
Mon 26	Saint Stephens Day Boxing Day	#StStephensDay #BoxingDay
Tue 27	National Fruitcake Day	#NationalFruitcakeDay
Wed 28	Card Playing Day National Download Day	#CardPlayingDay #NationalDownloadDay
Thur 29	National Pepper Pot Day	#PepperPotDay
Fri 30	National Bacon Day	#NationalBaconDay
Sat 31	New Years Eve	#NYE

DECEMBER 2022

Sun	Mon	Tue	Wed	Thu	Fri	Sat
				01	02	03
04	05	06	07	08	09	10
11	12	13	14	15	16	17
18	19	20	21	22	23	24
25	26	27	28	29	30	31

> Notes

JANUARY 2022

> Monday 3

IRE, UK - New Year's Day

> Tuesday 4

> Wednesday 5

WEEK 1

> Thursday 6

> Friday 7

> Saturday 8

> Sunday 9

JANUARY 2022

> Monday 10

> Tuesday 11

> Wednesday 12

WEEK 2

> Thursday 13

> Friday 14

> Saturday 15

> Sunday 16

JANUARY 2022

> Monday 17

US - Martin Luther King Jr. Day

> Tuesday 18

> Wednesday 19

WEEK 3

> Thursday 20

> Friday 21

> Saturday 22

> Sunday 23

JANUARY 2022

> Monday 24

> Tuesday 25

> Wednesday 26

WEEK 4

> Thursday 27

> Friday 28

> Saturday 29

> Sunday 30

 **LouiseMcDonnell**

JANUARY / FEBRUARY 2022

> Monday 31 January

> Tuesday 1 February

> Wednesday 2

WEEK 5

> Thursday 3

> Friday 4

> Saturday 5

> Sunday 6

FEBRUARY 2022

> Monday 07

> Tuesday 08

> Wednesday 09

WEEK 6

> Thursday 10

> Friday 11

> Saturday 12

> Sunday 13

FEBRUARY 2022

> Monday 14

> Tuesday 15

> Wednesday 16

WEEK 7

> Thursday 17

> Friday 18

> Saturday 19

> Sunday 20

FEBRUARY 2022

> Monday 21

> Tuesday 22

> Wednesday 23

WEEK 8

> Thursday 24

> Friday 25

> Saturday 26

> Sunday 27

FEBRUARY / MARCH 2022

> Monday 28 February

> Tuesday 01 March

> Wednesday 02

WEEK 9

> Thursday 03

> Friday 04

> Saturday 05

> Sunday 06

MARCH 2022

> Monday 07

> Tuesday 08

> Wednesday 09

WEEK 10

> Thursday 10

> Friday 11

> Saturday 12

> Sunday 13

MARCH 2022

> Monday 14

> Tuesday 15

> Wednesday 16

WEEK 11

> Thursday 17

IRE - St Patrick's Day

> Friday 18

> Saturday 19

> Sunday 20

MARCH 2022

> Monday 21

> Tuesday 22

> Wednesday 23

WEEK 12

> Thursday 24

> Friday 25

> Saturday 26

> Sunday 27

MARCH / APRIL 2022

> Monday 28

> Tuesday 29

> Wednesday 30

WEEK 13

> Thursday 31

> Friday 01 April

> Saturday 02

> Sunday 03

APRIL 2022

> Monday 04

> Tuesday 05

> Wednesday 06

WEEK 14

> Thursday 07

> Friday 08

> Saturday 09

> Sunday 10

APRIL 2022

> Monday 11

> Tuesday 12

> Wednesday 13

WEEK 15

> Thursday 14

> Friday 15

UK - Good Friday

> Saturday 16

> Sunday 17

APRIL 2022

> Monday 18

IRE, UK - Easter Monday

> Tuesday 19

> Wednesday 20

WEEK 16

> Thursday 21

> Friday 22

> Saturday 23

> Sunday 24

APRIL / MAY 2022

> Monday 25

> Tuesday 26

> Wednesday 27

WEEK 17

> Thursday 28

> Friday 29

> Saturday 30

> Sunday 01 May

MAY 2022

> Monday 02

IRE, UK - Early Bank Holiday Monday

> Tuesday 03

> Wednesday 04

WEEK 18

> Thursday 05

> Friday 06

> Saturday 07

> Sunday 08

MAY 2022

> Monday 09

> Tuesday 10

> Wednesday 11

WEEK 19

> Thursday 12

> Friday 13

> Saturday 14

> Sunday 15

MAY 2022

> Monday 16

> Tuesday 17

> Wednesday 18

WEEK 20

> Thursday 19

> Friday 20

> Saturday 21

> Sunday 22

MAY 2022

> Monday 23

> Tuesday 24

> Wednesday 25

WEEK 21

> Thursday 26

> Friday 27

> Saturday 28

> Sunday 29

MAY / JUNE 2022

> ### Monday 30 May

US - Memorial Day

> ### Tuesday 31

> ### Wednesday 01 June

WEEK 22

> **Thursday 02**

UK - Spring Bank Holiday

> **Friday 03**

UK - Platinum Jubilee Bank Holiday

> Saturday 04

> Sunday 05

JUNE 2022

> Monday 06

IRE, UK - June Bank Holiday

> Tuesday 07

> Wednesday 08

WEEK 23

> Thursday 09

> Friday 10

> Saturday 11

> Sunday 12

JUNE 2022

> Monday 13

> Tuesday 14

> Wednesday 15

WEEK 24

> Thursday 16

> Friday 17

> Saturday 18

> Sunday 19

JUNE 2022

> Monday 20

> Tuesday 21

> Wednesday 22

WEEK 25

> Thursday 23

> Friday 24

> Saturday 25

> Sunday 26

JUNE / JULY 2022

> Monday 27

> Tuesday 28

> Wednesday 29

WEEK 26

> Thursday 30

> Friday 01 July

> Saturday 02

> Sunday 03

JULY 2022

> Monday 04

US - Independence Day

> Tuesday 05

> Wednesday 06

WEEK 27

> Thursday 07

> Friday 08

> Saturday 09

> Sunday 10

JULY 2022

> Monday 11

> Tuesday 12

> Wednesday 13

WEEK 28

> Thursday 14

> Friday 15

> Saturday 16

> Sunday 17

JULY 2022

> Monday 18

> Tuesday 19

> Wednesday 20

WEEK 29

> Thursday 21

> Friday 22

> Saturday 23

> Sunday 24

JULY 2022

> Monday 25

> Tuesday 26

> Wednesday 27

WEEK 30

> Thursday 28

> Friday 29

> Saturday 30

> Sunday 31

AUGUST 2022

> Monday 01

IRE - August Bank Holiday

> Tuesday 02

> Wednesday 03

WEEK 31

> Thursday 04

> Friday 05

> Saturday 06

> Sunday 07

AUGUST 2022

> Monday 08

> Tuesday 09

> Wednesday 10

WEEK 32

> Thursday 11

> Friday 12

> Saturday 13

> Sunday 14

AUGUST 2022

> Monday 15

> Tuesday 16

> Wednesday 17

WEEK 33

> Thursday 18

> Friday 19

> Saturday 20

> Sunday 21

AUGUST 2022

> Monday 22

> Tuesday 23

> Wednesday 24

WEEK 34

> Thursday 25

> Friday 26

> Saturday 27

> Sunday 28

Louise McDonnell

AUGUST / SEPTEMBER 2022

> Monday 29 August

UK - Summer Bank Holiday

> Tuesday 30

> Wednesday 31

WEEK 35

> Thursday 01 September

> Friday 02

> Saturday 03

> Sunday 04

SEPTEMBER 2022

> Monday 05

US - Labor Day

> Tuesday 06

> Wednesday 07

WEEK 36

> Thursday 08

> Friday 09

> Saturday 10

> Sunday 11

SEPTEMBER 2022

> Monday 12

> Tuesday 13

> Wednesday 14

WEEK 37

> Thursday 15

> Friday 16

> Saturday 17

> Sunday 18

SEPTEMBER 2022

> Monday 19

> Tuesday 20

> Wednesday 21

WEEK 38

> Thursday 22

> Friday 23

> Saturday 24

> Sunday 25

SEPTEMBER / OCTOBER 2022

> Monday 26

> Tuesday 27

> Wednesday 28

WEEK 39

> Thursday 29

> Friday 30

> Saturday 01 October

> Sunday 02

OCTOBER 2022

> Monday 03

> Tuesday 04

> Wednesday 05

WEEK 40

> Thursday 06

> Friday 07

> Saturday 08

> Sunday 09

OCTOBER 2022

> Monday 10

> Tuesday 11

> Wednesday 12

WEEK 41

> Thursday 13

> Friday 14

> Saturday 15

> Sunday 16

OCTOBER 2022

> Monday 17

> Tuesday 18

> Wednesday 19

WEEK 42

> Thursday 20

> Friday 21

> Saturday 22

> Sunday 23

OCTOBER 2022

> Monday 24

> Tuesday 25

> Wednesday 26

WEEK 43

> Thursday 27

> Friday 28

> Saturday 29

> Sunday 30

OCTOBER / NOVEMBER 2022

> Monday 31 October

IRE - October Bank Holiday

> Tuesday 01 November

> Wednesday 02

WEEK 44

> Thursday 03

> Friday 04

> Saturday 05

> Sunday 06

NOVEMBER 2022

> Monday 07

> Tuesday 08

> Wednesday 09

WEEK 45

> Thursday 10

> Friday 11

US - Veterans Day

> Saturday 12

> Sunday 13

NOVEMBER 2022

> Monday 14

> Tuesday 15

> Wednesday 16

WEEK 46

> Thursday 17

> Friday 18

> Saturday 19

> Sunday 20

NOVEMBER 2022

> Monday 21

> Tuesday 22

> Wednesday 23

WEEK 47

> Thursday 24

US - Thanksgiving

> Friday 25

> Saturday 26

> Sunday 27

NOVEMBER / DECEMBER 2022

> Monday 28 November

> Tuesday 29

> Wednesday 30

WEEK 48

> Thursday 01 December

> Friday 02

> Saturday 03

> Sunday 04

DECEMBER 2022

> Monday 05

> Tuesday 06

> Wednesday 07

WEEK 49

> Thursday 08

> Friday 09

> Saturday 10

> Sunday 11

DECEMBER 2022

> Monday 12

> Tuesday 13

> Wednesday 14

WEEK 50

> Thursday 15

> Friday 16

> Saturday 17

> Sunday 18

DECEMBER 2022

> Monday 19

> Tuesday 20

> Wednesday 21

WEEK 51

> Thursday 22

> Friday 23

> Saturday 24

> Sunday 25

IRE - Christmas Day / UK - Christmas Day / US - Christmas Day

DECEMBER 2022

> Monday 26

IRE - St Stephen's Day / UK - Boxing Day

> Tuesday 27

> Wednesday 28

WEEK 52

> Thursday 29

> Friday 30

> Saturday 31

> Sunday 01 January 2023